Faith on the Edge Series

The Unexplained
Miracles, Mysteries, and More

Christopher Halbert

CONCORDIA PUBLISHING HOUSE · SAINT LOUIS

3   4   5   6   7   8   9   10   11   12   14 13 12 11 10 09 08 07 06 05

CONTENTS

About This Series

In the past, science served as a stepchild of alchemy, a handmaiden of theology, and a tool of industry. At the beginning of the twentieth century, science took on a new role. Science became the answer to all humankind's problems. The priests and priestesses of science pulled on their white lab coats, prophesied through their theories, and consecrated each new discovery or invention. Humans marveled.

In response to these new inventions, a new type of literature arose—science fiction, which sometimes warned us about the maddening pace of technology. The robot would replace the human worker. Nuclear fallout would devastate life on earth. Science would solve people's problems by doing away with people, or at least by doing away with their humanity.

Today, people remain thankful for science. But they also recognize that science does not hold all the answers. In fact, they see that science can raise more questions than it answers, driving people on further quests for understanding, truth, and contentment.

The Faith on the Edge Bible study series tracks the progress of science and people's fascinations and fears about science. Each session introduces a contemporary topic, summarizes what science has to say about it, and then provides biblical answers and guidance so that you can face the future with the wisdom and confidence that only God can provide.

Student Introduction

Teacher, we want to see a miraculous sign from you.

—Some Pharisees and teachers of the Law (Matthew 12:38)

This Bible study is not merely an "encounter" with strange encounters, but a tool for discerning the truth with a Christ-centered mind. The first session on miracles is not meant to be a "Ripley's Believe It or Not" that woos onlookers and creates senseless wonder. It shows that miracles have a set purpose. They focus on Christ. God's redemptive purposes are revealed through the miraculous deeds that reach their culmination in the person and work of Christ. Therefore, this study calls you to be Christ-minded, seeing persons and events in this life in relationship to Christ.

The first session also shows that miracles really happen. Understanding miracles allows one to consider other metaphysical topics (metaphysics refers to one's beliefs about reality). For example, if God can intervene in history with a miraculous deed, then life is more than "natural." It is supernatural. God is present in history.

Most importantly, miracles are not distant or transcendent events. God does not come from behind a "heavenly curtain," perform a miracle as a magic trick to shock us, and then go "backstage" and remain there. Miracles are personal. Dr. Martin Luther liked to emphasize that God's works are *pro me*, or "for me." God is a God "for me," or as Christians say in the Nicene Creed, "for us," because He performs miraculous deeds for our salvation and brings us to faith in Him. God is close or immanent in a relational sense. This immanence is revealed chiefly in Jesus Christ. Thus, miracles and other supernatural causes are not only meant for us to "look above" to the Divine, but also to "look below" to the baby at Bethlehem and His miraculous work. In Christ, we see both the "above" and the "below" because He is God in human flesh.

The Gospel Principle

This study of unexplained phenomena will leave you with a lot of things unexplained—that seems to be a given. However, you will also find a common appeal in this Bible study to something I call "The Gospel-principle." This principle helps Christians discern the truth about the unexplained things in life. For example, if I am wondering whether a certain miracle or teaching is from God, I *first* judge it in light of the Gospel by asking, "Does the event support or undermine the teaching of the Gospel?"

False teachings and false miracles ultimately come from the devil. If we are to defeat him we must oppose the purpose of such falsehoods. The purpose of the devil's lies and deceptions is to keep us from salvation in Christ. The fires of the devil are extinguished by the waters of Christ in Baptism. To discern whether a teaching opposes the teaching of Christ and His salvation, one must compare it with the Gospel message. One can use this "rule of faith" as a starting point.

At the same time, the Gospel does not give us answers for *everything*. God has given us the gift of reason for discerning matters involving science, math, morality, and other daily affairs. But, when there is an event or teaching occurring in God's name within Christendom, or under a Christian name, then we should judge it appropriately.

May Christ guide you by the Gospel as you use this study. Amen.

Christopher Halbert

CHAPTER ONE

Miracles

Miracle Service—Every Tuesday

—a message on a church marquee

The possibility of miracles fascinates people. A *Reader's Digest* article told of a miracle occurring right after Christmas one year. That Christmas, Arthur Stevens received from his daughter a handy, waterproof flashlight like the kind he had always wanted. Nearly a month later, he went out to sea on the tugboat, Harkness, with a friend and the captain, Rudy Musetti.

During their trip, a violent storm erupted and the boat began taking on water. With winds blowing up to 40 mph, the crew found itself in grave danger. Captain Musetti radioed for help as they began to sink. Three lobstermen heard the message, and set out to search for them. As the lobstermen searched, they saw a beam of light. The flashlight Stevens received as a Christmas present had froze to his friend's glove in the icy water. Its beam shone upward, leading the rescuers to the men of the *Harkness*! The flashlight saved their lives.

1. Has a remarkable event similar to this one ever occurred in your life? If so, do you think that it was directly caused by God? Can such events be explained in another way?

2. Read Exodus 6:1–8; 9:16; 14:31. What do these verses say about the purpose of miracles? Moreover, what do they teach about the relationship between faith and miracles?

6:1-8 - God said I will free the Jews from slavery in Egypt

9:16 - God sent a hail storm to kill the crops & the animals of the Egyptians but save those of the Jews

14:31 He dried the river for the Jews to cross & let the river rush in & drown the Egyptians

3. In the destruction of the World Trade Center, some people miraculously survived, while others tragically died. Should we say that the survivors had God's favor upon them? If so, what should we say about those who suffered and died?

4. In John 11 Jesus allowed His friend Lazarus to remain ill and even to die. Read John 11:3–15 and reflect on Jesus' words and actions. What can they teach you about miracles and tragic events today?

Doubts about Miracles

The eighteenth century philosopher David Hume stated in his treatise, *An Inquiry Concerning Human Understanding*, that miracles violate the laws of nature. For Hume and other Enlightenment thinkers, human experience is the final criterion of truth. Experience proved the laws of nature and disproved miracles. In other words, the discovery of the laws of nature did away with the need for miracles. (For more on Naturalism, see p. 79 in Glossary.)

However, David Hume also pointed out that the traditional Christian definition of a miracle is something that occurs *outside* of the regular course of events. To understand Hume's point, we need to distinguish between something being *against* another thing and something being *outside* of another thing.

Consider the following. A fire set beneath a pan of water will heat the water even though the fire and water never touch one another. They are outside of one another. If you dumped the water onto the fire, that would heat the water too. But in that case, the items would mingle with one another. They would be against one another.

A miracle is an *extra*-ordinary event; that is, it is something *outside* of the regular course of nature. For example, when God parted the Red Sea, gravity did not cease to exist. He did not extinguish the laws of nature. He merely acted outside the natural laws in parting the sea.

With this point in mind, recognize that Mr. Hume's arguments against miracles do not address the same issue. He argued against miracles that *violate* natural law. In contrast, the Christian position asserts that miracles are *outside* of natural law. Hume's famous argument does not really address the miracles described by a Christian at all!

5. Can science prove or disprove miracles? Why or why not?

Many skeptics toward Christianity deny the existence of miracles because they believe that miracles go against the laws of nature explained by science. They assert that if events violate or are not explained by natural laws, these events must not have really occurred.

This is certainly a cavalier assertion. Theodore Handrich explains in his book, *Everyday Science for the Christian,* how natural laws do not cause things to happen. Natural Laws simply describe things that ordinarily happen. Therefore, natural laws do not cause the events in the world around us, but are related to them as a journalist is to news events.

Remember that natural law employed by science does not determine what *can* happen. It describes what *usually* happens in the course of nature. In other words, since natural law describes events that *regularly* occur, it leaves open the possibility that something else may occur. And, if it were something of a miraculous nature, then science would not dismiss its occurrence, but simply be left "scratching its head" because of such an event.

6. Read about the scientific method on pp.77–78. What kind of knowledge does science present to us?

7. How does Scripture describe God's relationship to the world (Genesis 1:1–27; Psalm 50:1–6; Matthew 6:25–34)?

Miracles and Manipulation

For centuries people have sought signs or miracles. During Jesus' ministry, the Jewish religious leaders demanded that He show them His miraculous power. Christ rebuked them stating, "A wicked and adulterous generation asks for a miraculous sign! But none will be given it except the sign of the prophet Jonah" (Matthew 12:39).

Jesus, of course, was not against performing miracles. But He rebuked the religious leaders of His day because of their motives in asking for miracles. They requested miracles in order to test Him without any sincere intent to follow Him. They also disconnected miracles from the promises of God's Word. Christ rebuked them by alluding to His resurrection: "For as Jonah was three days and three nights in the belly of a huge fish, so the Son of Man will be three days and three nights in the heart of the earth" (Matthew 12:40).

8. Why do people crave miracles? Read Deuteronomy 29:29. What does Scripture say about speculating beyond the things that God has revealed?

People today test God by crying out that they will follow Him if He does something miraculous before their eyes. For example, people point to the many miracles recorded in the Book of Acts and suggest that God ought to be doing such miracles now. The Lord gives very different reasons for us to follow Him. God does not urge us to test His ability to do miracles. He invites us to test His Word and deeds. The Lord calls us to believe in Him based on whether His testimony is actually confirmed in historical reality (Deuteronomy 18:21–22; John 14:11). Thus, the Word of God is our source of truth. The ultimate action confirming its truthfulness is the resurrection of Christ (Acts 2:30–32; 3:15, 18; 17:31).

Moreover, remember that the miracles occurring in the Book of Acts are not some grand "miracle-parade," which Christians must experience each day. They are done over the first 20 years of the Church's mission work. God did these miracles not only to demonstrate His presence but also to bring people to a saving faith in Christ in His resurrection (John 14:11; Acts 2:22).

9. The mighty acts of God have been open to human observation. Does that mean we can understand them? Why or why not? Read Job 37:5.

10. Understanding the miracles recorded in Scripture can be challenging. What caution should this provide for us when we consider remarkable events not recorded in Scripture?

Most likely you have heard of the television evangelists claiming that they have healed people of many terminal diseases or other ailments. I remember driving by one church that advertised on its marquee: "Miracle Service—Every Tuesday." A planned miracle-service seems ridiculous. Personal claims of miraculous power seem bogus. Aren't miracles spontaneous?! How can any mere person plan a miracle? God is the one who plans and initiates miracles, and on His own terms! Moreover, we must watch out for false miracles. Scripture warns that the devil has the capacity for creating miracles to delude people and direct them away from the truth. Furthermore, Scripture warns that God will allow such false miracles to occur as a result of His judgment (2 Thessalonians 2:9–12).

11. Many people reason, "The disciples of Jesus did miracles. If a religious leader can perform miracles today, he must be a disciple of Jesus." What's wrong with this reasoning? Read Matthew 24:24 and Revelation 13:11–14a.

12. Why should the Gospel be the specific rule for measuring whether a miracle done in Christ's name is true or not, and not Scripture in a general sense? Read Matthew 4:5–7.

The Lord of Miracles

Miracles have a two-fold purpose: (1) to manifest God's glory and Name before humankind; (2) to create faith in those observing the miracles. It may be noted that this is not an "either/or." God can do miracles for the purpose of revealing His Name to both believers as well as to unbelievers (Exodus 9:16; 1 Kings 18:38–39; Isaiah 25:1–5). But, it is important to remember that miracles do, indeed, have a salvific purpose behind them. Many of the miracles of both the Old and New Testament confirm this (Exodus 14:31; Psalm 105: 26–45; John 11:38–42; 14:11).

Although we are darkened in our minds by sin and may have trusted in false miracles before, God has mercy on us in Jesus Christ. Remember, by faith in Christ, you have been brought from the kingdom of darkness to His very own kingdom of grace and forgiveness (Colossians 1:13). You have been given faith which overcomes Satan's kingdom of delusion and brings you into favor with God (Romans 5:11; 1 John 4:4). Indeed, God has miraculously intervened in human history in Jesus Christ, not only to grant you faith, but also to purchase salvation for you through His death and resurrection (Romans 3:23–26; 4:24–25).

13. Reflect on the celebration of Easter in your life and the life of your congregation. How important is the resurrection for your personal faith?

The resurrection is the ultimate miracle of God not only because it is the basis of salvation, but also because it verifies God's promises for us. Because Christ has defeated death, we have hope. He has opened the gates of heaven to us, that we might be glorified with Him (1 Corinthians 15:54–57; John 11:25–26). Moreover, in a world of ambiguity and fakery, we can have certainty that God has maintained His promises by fulfilling them in the risen Christ. Christ's defeat of death not only bears witness to the truthfulness of God's promises, but also to the certainty of having hope that we too will be raised unto glory!

And your faith is not only a miracle itself, but a miracle that participates in greater miracles—the person and work of Jesus Christ (2 Peter 1:3–4). Moreover, we need not look for miracles outside the Word and Sacraments. God works miracles through the Word by leading us to repentance and renewing us in His image. He works miracles in Baptism and the Lord's Supper by forgiving our sins and causing us to be born again!

14. Read Matthew 12:38–40; Romans 6:4; 1 Corinthians 15:1–11. What importance does God place on the resurrection with respect to faith?

15. Read John 5:28–29; 11:25–26; Romans 6:5–11. How can the miracle of the resurrection benefit you today?

Words to Remember

We were therefore buried with him through Baptism into death in order that, just as Christ was raised from the dead through the glory of the Father, we too may live a new life. Romans 6:4

Mystical Experiences

I n 1999, the film *Stigmata* drew millions of people to movie theaters. It was inspired by the mystical experiences of the medieval friar, St. Francis of Assisi. "Stigmata" refers to the miraculous appearance of the five wounds of Christ upon a person's body. Although the film is fictional, St. Francis's stigmata supposedly has a historical basis. In fact, similar events have been recorded by people interested in mystical experiences.

Reportedly, St. Francis was the first to receive the stigmata. According to the story, after forty days of fasting and prayer, St. Francis proceeded up a mountain to reflect upon the death and suffering of Jesus. While he was contemplating Jesus' suffering, Jesus appeared and granted St. Francis "copies" of His own wounds.

In contrast to the story of St. Francis, the film *Stigmata* has as its main character an agnostic, young suburban hairdresser who has been "divinely chosen" to receive the stigmata. She undergoes a series of traumatic experiences while receiving the "copies" of Christ's wounds. The miraculous wounds send her into euphoric states of shock and confusion. Although the young woman was an unbeliever, God ordained that she receive the stigmata as a powerful introduction to the spiritual realities of life. The film contrasts the corruption of organized religion with the genuineness of mystical experience, a theme that is increasingly popular in contemporary culture.

16. Give other examples of mystical experiences you've heard about. How important are these stories/experiences for shaping your life and beliefs?

17. Read Acts 9:1–9. How does St. Paul's experience compare and contrast with the experience of St. Francis?

Evaluating Experiences

In his book, *Looking for a Miracle: Weeping Icons, Relics, Stigmata, Visions and Healing Cures*, Joe Nickell mentions that medieval Christians were fascinated with the physical suffering of Christ and the wounds affected upon His body at the Crucifixion. They engaged in morbid curiosity regarding the passion of our Lord. There are some reported cases of people purposefully inflicting themselves with wounds similar to those of Christ's as a way of copying His example in submitting to God's will by His death on a cross. Nickell describes such cases as examples of fraudulent stigmatics. His research revealed many cases. Quite often, fake stigmatics injured themselves in a state of mental illness.

In some parts of the world, a similar fascination continues today. For example, at an Easter festival in the Philippines, penitents undergo crucifixion for several hours. But Christians are not the only people who seek greater identification with a religious figure through suffering. Many Shia Muslims whip themselves bloody at the end of the festival of Ashura in order to identify more closely with the sufferings of Imam Ali, the son-in-law of Muhammad. Other examples of self-inflicted suffering for religious purposes include the sun dance of the Sioux Indians and the piercing and suspension rituals practiced by some Hindus.

18. Another type of mystical experience involves people who claim that Jesus appeared to them. Have you ever encountered anyone who claimed to have received a direct revelation from the risen Christ? If so, how did that person describe their experience?

Prior to the ascension, Christ had not undergone any outward transformation in His body, (glorification as in 1 Corinthians 15:52–54; Philippians 3:21). Part of the reason for this was to establish the validity of His resurrected body and to impart clear evidence that He truly had risen bodily from the dead (Acts 1:1–3). St. Paul, however, encountered the glorified Christ (note Jesus' appearance with bright light in Acts 9:3). After the ascension, this was the only way Christ appeared to people. This distinction may be significant when considering people's claims that they have had direct encounters with Christ. Many people experiencing discouragement or suffering claim they saw Christ in an *un-glorified* manner. Such experiences don't seem to fit with the appearances of Christ—post-ascension—as described in Scripture.

19. Read Philippians 1:27–30 and 1 Peter 4:12–16. In these passages, how do the apostles encourage Christians who face suffering?

Researcher Ian Wilson has suggested that cases such as St. Francis's could simply have been a result of his extreme fasting. The friar's mental state could have led to self-inflicted wounds in light of his probable fascination with the crucifixion.

Twentieth century Roman Catholic priest Padre Pio serves as a more modern case of reported stigmatics. Evidently, Padre Pio received the wounds of Christ for several years. It was also reported that he could remain alert for 18 hours a day, listening to people's confessions. His experiences and his commitment to serving people by hearing their confessions of sin created an enormous following.

Oddly when Padre Pio died, the wounds of the stigmata on his body could not be found. No scars or traces of self-inflicted wounds appeared on his hands and feet. Researchers have suggested that it may be possible for stigmata to occur through *psychosomatic* means. In other words, as a result of intense concentration and mental conviction the mind could cause wounds upon the body—a person might actually concentrate so hard on receiving the wounds that such wounds might appear!

If this is the case, the wounds of Padre Pio are little different from the self-inflicted wounds of other stigmatics, or anyone who uses suffering as a means to gain a mystical experience.

God Works through Means

20. Read John 14:23–24; 1 Corinthians 11:23–26; and 1 John 4:9–10. How do we maintain a proper understanding of Christ and the centrality of His Cross?

Mystical experiences emphasize what theologians call *immediate* revelation, or revelation that does not come through *means*. *Means* refer to those things which God uses as instruments to reveal and present Himself to us. For example, both God's Word and the Sacraments of Baptism and the Lord's Supper are means because God uses them to reveal His will and to be present with His people.

Mystical experiences seek God in a direct or immediate way apart from the use of Word or Sacrament.

One could argue that false stigmatics misuse the crucifixion of Christ. Certainly, the cross represents a central point of Christian faith. But Jesus never intended that we repeat His crucifixion in our own bodies. Rather, the cross is presented in Scripture as the basis of both our justification and our sanctification (Romans 3:24–26; 5:9; 6:6–14; 1 Peter 4:1–2).

21. Read Genesis 3:8 and note how Adam and Eve perceived God's presence. Also read Exodus 3:1–5; 33:9–11, 20–23. In these passages, what are the different ways in which God revealed Himself to humankind? What do these passages tell us about the nature of God and how He reveals Himself?

We must acknowledge that, because of our sin, God is unapproachable apart from mediation or means. God is holy, He dwells in "unapproachable light" (1 Timothy 6:16). A person cannot approach God apart from the mediating work of Jesus Christ (John 14:6; Romans 5:10). Even though there is a temptation in each one of us to make personal experience our basis for knowing God, we should resist such temptation. God provides His Word and Sacraments as ways of "experiencing" Him.

Looking for truth in experience, or from within, is dangerous. The Word tells us, "the heart is deceitful above all things" (Jeremiah 17:9). If we rely on our own hearts and opinions as a normative source for truth, we will rely on a shaky and faulty foundation. But, if we look to the Word as an objective standard for truth, we will have a firm and solid foundation (John 17:17).

22. Read John 6:63. Even though God is physically unapproachable, in what ways does God become present for us?

23. Read Matthew 6:9–13. What is the purpose for prayer presented in Jesus' words? Does prayer point us to a revelation apart from God's Word or to a revelation in keeping with God's Word?

God's Gracious Gifts Found through Means

God comes to us in forms of mediation, presenting His gracious gifts of forgiveness and salvation. Because these means lack outward extravagance, we may find ourselves looking to things other than Word and Sacrament to find God. But ironically, what God provides for us contains dynamic and life-giving qualities.

For example, when you partake of the body and blood of Christ at the Lord's Table, you are partaking of the life-giving elements of the risen Savior. Faith, inspired by Christ, is truly a dynamic thing because it participates in Christ as its object and lays hold of "the bread" that Christ gives "for the life of the world" (John 6:51).

Moreover, when God comes to you through means, He is doing this because He loves you. By God coming to you through Word and Sacrament, He is coming to you in such a way that is "safe," and giving you an opportunity to experience His presence for your benefit rather than for your harm. For God to abide with us through forms of mediation is a witness to His unfailing love. God could have abandoned His creation and remained transcendent. And we would never come to know Him. But, the heavenly Father, in His love, chose to reconcile you unto Himself by sending the one true mediator, Jesus Christ (Ephesians 1:5–7; 1 Timothy 2:5; Romans 5:10–11).

24. How would you describe the state of your faith-relationship with Christ?

25. Read 1 John 4:9–10; Titus 3:4–7. What things bring us to remembrance of God's love for us in spite of our sins?

Words
to Remember

All this is from God, who reconciled us to Himself through Christ and gave us the ministry of reconciliation. 2 Corinthians 5:18

Near-Death Experiences

W hen Holly went to the hospital for carpal-tunnel surgery, she couldn't have anticipated the surprising events of that day. During surgery, Holly experienced a violent seizure in reaction to a medication. Despite the efforts of doctors and nurses, Holly died. Suddenly, she heard a beatific voice. She saw no one, but heard the voice telling her that she could come away with the person speaking to her or she could come later. She did not know exactly what was happening. She felt blissful. She responded to the voice, saying that she had to go back because she wanted to continue taking care of her family and her responsibilities as a mother and wife. At that point, the doctors resuscitated Holly. She remains alive today and remembers her experience, believing that it was God Himself who spoke to her. She attributes the peace she experienced in that event to the promise of salvation God has provided in Jesus Christ.

Not every near-death experience is so peaceful. For example, a young man involved in a horrible auto accident was brought to an emergency room. In a state of incoherence, he suddenly felt himself rising up. He looked around and saw the hospital room. He looked down and saw a body that had lost two of its limbs. He felt sorry for the person who had been disfigured. But, it soon occurred to him that he was looking at his very own body. He believed that he had passed out of his body and had been separated from it.

26. Have you ever talked with someone who has had a near-death experience? What was their experience like?

Modern Research

M any people discount any possibility of near-death experiences because they believe in only naturalism rather than supernatural causes. Some regard these experiences as the result of psychological illnesses, side effects from medications, or as mere dreams.

Yet another reason for denying near-death experiences comes from nihilistic assumptions. Nihilism is the philosophical belief that life has no meaning. For the Nihilist, nothing happens when a person dies. That person merely ceases to exist. The nihilist believes that when a person dies, they do not experience an afterlife, nor have any conscious awareness of anything, because there is nothing existing outside of this life.

27. What do you think of the philosophical positions of naturalism and nihilism with regard to near-death experiences? Do you think they offer sufficient explanations against near-death experiences?

A Gallup study estimated in 1982 that nearly 8 million people in the United States have had a near-death experience. The poll was subdivided into the different types of near-death experiences people had. The most common experiences reported were visitations to another dimension, life reviews, feelings of bliss, out of body experiences, and encounters with other beings.

28. Do the numbers of near-death experiences prove the validity of such experiences? Why or why not?

Near-death experiences are usually argued to be the result of three major types of mental illnesses: schizophrenia, delirium, and autoscopic hallucinations. Researcher Raymond Moody has carefully researched near-death experiences and argued that they are not the result of psychological or mental illnesses. Moody offers substantial explanations to refute each of these claims.

Moody notes that near-death experiences contradict many traits of schizophrenia. For example, schizophrenics usually cannot function in society and lead a life of isolation, while most people who have had near-death experiences cope with society better after their experience than they did before it. They are characterized by love and peace, and function better in the world around them. Fundamentally, the effects of the near-death experience are positive, while the effects of schizophrenia are negative.

Near-death experiences are also not caused by delirium. Delirium results from a significant chemical imbalance in the brain, which causes disjointed thought patterns or even random hallucinations. A near-death experience is characterized by lucid and coherent perception. Moody describes how people suffering from delirium observe images in an impersonal or detached manner, as if they were watching them on a movie screen. A near-death experience, however, is usually described in a highly detailed and personal manner.

Finally, there is the claim that near-death experiences are actually autoscopic hallucinations. *Autoscopic hallucinations* are when a person sees himself or herself in a third-person manner (i.e., their double), but is aware that this other "them," their double, is a separate distinct person. Moody notes that these hallucinations are only from the perspective of one's own physical body, and are therefore limited. In contrast, people with out-of-body experiences have a solid perception of their own body and are able to float or roam around to observe places their body could not occupy. The entire time the person recognizes their body as theirs and not that of another person or "double." The essential difference is that a person undergoing an out-of-body experience holds a totally different center of perception than the one with a hallucination.

29. What do you think of Moody's arguments? Do they refute proposed explanations of near-death experiences?

Death as a Result of the Fall

A discussion about near-death experiences, of course, presupposes the reality of death. God's Word does not specifically explain much about near-death experiences. But since the discussion involves death, we must consider the cause of death: sin.

Scripture tells us, "God made mankind upright, but men have gone in search of many schemes" (Ecclesiastes 7:29). When God created Adam and Eve, they lived in a state of perfect righteousness, enjoying peaceful fellowship with God where there was no death. The command God gave Adam and Eve was to abstain from eating from the tree of the knowledge of good and evil in the middle of the garden. For if they ate from that tree, death would result (Genesis 2:17). By disobeying God's command, Adam and Eve brought spiritual and physical death to themselves and their posterity (Romans 5:12). Moreover, disorder resulted from their sin.

Medieval theologian Thomas Aquinas noted how the fall resulted in the disorder of human reason and will. People no longer live with unified purpose, thinking and willing what is right. They often place what is wrong ahead of what they know to be right. The disorder resulting from the fall has resulted in an unnatural separation between body and soul, which we call "death."

Martin Luther made special note of this in his treatise,

Confession Concerning Christ's Supper. Luther maintained that the body and soul are in essential unity. Where the body is present, there the soul is present along with it. However, because of the fall, the essential unity between body and soul has been changed, resulting in their separation at death. This view allows for the fact that even though someone is buried, his or her soul exists in an afterlife.

30. Read 2 Corinthians 5:1–8; Philippians 1:22–24. How do these passages describe the relationship between the soul and the body at the point of death?

The separation of body and soul is the mournful consequence of the first sin. God tells us that He gave the commandments so that we may have life. In Eden, God gave Adam His commandments to show him the way of life and to prevent him from hurting himself. Adam, with Eve's encouragement, chose to disobey God and brought this burden of death upon us all.

31. Read Romans 5:12–19. Do you think that it is unfair that all of humankind should bear the effects of death from one man's sin?

32. Read Acts 7:54–60. Some might regard Stephen's experience as a near-death experience. Respond.

33. Based on John 11:11–14 and 1 Thessalonians 4:14–15, some people believe in *soul sleep*, that the soul or spirit does not conscious-

ly enjoy the presence of Christ or the bliss of heaven after a Christian dies. However, read Luke 16:19–31 and Revelation 6:9–10. What do these passages say about the state of the soul in death?

Christ the Lord of Life and Death

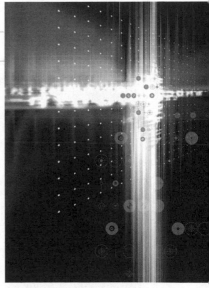

W hether or not you believe near-death experiences actually occur, two fundamental truths should be noted: (1) you will face God when you die, and (2) all people will die (unless God miraculously intervenes). Because of the separation of the soul and the body at death, the soul lives on while the body lies in the grave. Scripture tells us that the soul basically meets God in the world beyond, standing before Him in judgment. Christ, who holds the keys of Death and Hades (Revelation 1:18), is the only way to the kingdom of heaven (John 10:9; 14:6). Therefore one's entrance into either eternal condemnation or eternal life is ultimately based upon Christ.

Our Lord Jesus Christ knows our human weaknesses and even participated in human death. He died for you and for me, the ungodly, who were undeserving of such a sacrifice.

Christ is Lord over death, as His glorious resurrection shows. Such a victory has brought life to you, granting you the same hope of a bodily resurrection when Christ returns (Romans 6:9–10). Christ came to restore all things, including the disunity between our body and soul (John 5:25–29). You are redeemed from death by Christ. He promises to raise your physical body anew so that you may enjoy eternal life with Him as a whole person.

Because of the limits of science and because the Scriptures do not directly answer many of our questions about near-death experiences, such experiences remain unexplainable. No doubt, research and interest in this topic will continue. But instead of focusing on the unknown, focus on what you can know: peace through Christ.

34. Read Hebrews 4:14–16; 2 Corinthians 3:17–18. What do these passages assert about Christ and our faith-relationship with Him?

The Law condemns us under its demands. If the Law were the only covenant God gave us, there would be no hope. We would face God's wrath. But, the work of Christ delivers us from the condemnation of the Law, thereby delivering us from death's dominion.

Christ, who holds the power over death, brought you from death to life through faith (John 5:24; 8:51). Death no longer has mastery over you and you are now "more than conquerors" in Christ over death and its dominion (Romans 8:37). You have the hope of the resurrection in which you will be raised by Christ for future glory.

Death and resurrection are continual realities not only pertaining to Christ, but also pertaining to you. His death and resurrection provide the basis for your own personal death and resurrection. The Christian life you live is one of continual dying and rising. As Christians, Christ abides with you by faith. The death of Christ is your death because its effects are "credited to your account." The forgiveness of sins won at the cross was achieved on your behalf and freely given to you. Moreover, you are being renewed through the power of Christ and His Spirit, putting to death the sinful nature and recreating hearts and minds. The resurrection of Christ is your resurrection because, although it does not destroy the reality of physical death, it gives confidence and courage to face death knowing that the Lord Jesus Christ will raise you on the Last Day.

35. Read Romans 6:3–14. Note the themes of death and resurrection. Do you think that Christ's death and resurrection serves as the basis for your justification? Your sanctification? Both? Explain your answer.

Words
to Remember

The sting of death is sin, and the power of sin is the law. But thanks be to God! He gives us the victory through our Lord Jesus Christ. 1 Corinthians 15:56–57

CHAPTER FOUR

Dreams

N ew Age religious movements, such as Eckankar, and popular psychology have placed a great emphasis on dreams. This has led people to wonder what their dreams mean. Some wonder whether God is speaking to them through their dreams.

The Old Testament describes numerous dreams and their interpretation. For example, Joseph told his brothers of different bizarre dreams insinuating that he would have lordship over them and all his family.

36. Read Genesis 37:5–11, 18–20. Have you ever told friends or family of certain dreams that you have had? What was their reaction? How does our culture's view of dreams differ from the view expressed by Joseph's brothers?

Many Old Testament stories describe dreams given by God. For example, when Jacob went to sleep, he dreamed of a ladder coming from heaven. He saw angels surrounding the ladder and heard God promise land to him and his descendants. God promised Jacob and his descendants that they would inherit the very land he slept on, and that He would never forsake him (Genesis 28:11–16). To this day many Israelis consider this dream as evidence that God gave them the land of Israel. This dream and interpretation still affect issues of peace and conflict to this day!

Dreams and Their Interpretation

Psychologists have created a significant amount of research on dreams and their meanings. Sigmund Freud, the father of modern dream analysis, believed that dreams are symbols or representations of the inner sub-conscious. The inner sub-conscious is the compartment of the mind where man's innermost desires lie. Therefore, Freud concluded that dreams represent man's deepest desires.

37. Are all dreams directly from God or from our desires? Explain your opinion.

In a 1983 article of *The Journal of Psychology and Theology*, John Walsh described dreams as essentially symbolic. He asserted that dreams are symbolic realities that connect us with what is transcendent and otherwise unknown. He argued that dreams offer a certain Christological element by creating "incarnations" in our minds through concrete representations. In other words, spiritual things take a physical form when we dream. They communicate to us transcendent meanings through visions of physical images. Dreams connect us with the divine and transcendent.

38. What do you think of Walsh's theory about dreams connecting us with the divine? Explain your answer.

Walsh also gives an interpretation for St. Joseph's dream in Matthew 1:18–25. Walsh states that Matthew's account of Joseph's dream seems to come from a deep conviction that God works His will through dreams. It also suggests to him that Matthew had a personal experience of God in a dream.

Walsh goes on to suggest that Joseph's dream was a representation of his own desire for hero status. He maintains that Joseph's dream was the result of his own longing for status, filtered through his current cultural context of what was considered heroic.

39. Read Matthew 1:18–25. What do you think of Walsh's interpretation?

40. In view of Matthew's Gospel, what is Walsh's interpretation saying about the validity of Scripture? What are its implications for understanding Scripture?

Walsh also emphasizes the *archetypal* character of dreams for spirituality. He asserts that dreams present signs or patterns about the nature of a person's spiritual life. For Walsh, dreams can indicate the state of a person's relationship to God. A person can discern how God is working in their life through their dreams. Since dreams are a "pipeline" from the divine life to our own, they inform us about God's will as well as the nature of our faith.

41. Based on Matthew 1:18–25; Galatians 1:9–10. How may someone discern whether a dream is from God or not?

People in ancient times regarded dreams as a form of direct communication with the supernatural. For example, Egyptians and Mesopotamians held dreams in high status because they were more than likely forms of communication from the gods.

Dreams that come from pagan gods, or gods other than the One True God of Israel are essentially demonic. After all, such gods were set up and created by people as objects of worship, (idols). They were not real. Scripture mentions that demons will use such idols as "masks" and hide behind them, in a sense, leading people astray from worshiping the true God (1 Corinthians 10:19–20; Psalm 106:35–38). Therefore, one could maintain that dreams from supposed "gods" actually come from demons.

Empty Dreams

I f *all* dreams are revelations of God's will, then it would be safe to say that they have an authoritative status with regard to truth. Dreams then could be put on the same par with God's Word because they directly come from God. But, as has been shown, not all dreams come directly from God. Therefore, we should be discerning about our own dreams. We should not be too quick to use them as a normative source for truth.

42. Read Deuteronomy 18:19–22; Jeremiah 23:25–28. What do these passages say about false prophets?

People naturally look within to their ideas and feelings when they search for a standard for truth. In contrast, God urges us to look outside ourselves for truth. God's Word provides two important truths for guiding our lives: Law and Gospel. First, God proclaims His Law for our benefit. The Law shows us the true status of our sin and how we have forsaken His righteousness. The Law only benefits us if we keep it (Deuteronomy 6:3; Psalm 1; 119:1–8). The Law of God is good (1 Timothy 1:8) and an absolute standard of truth.

But the Law alone is not enough. The problem is that we naturally act against God's Law (Romans 3:10–20). Thus, we incur God's wrath (Ephesians 2:3; Isaiah 34:2; Malachi 1:10). The Lord shows us our utter failure to keep His Law and therefore shows us our need for a Savior in His Gospel (Romans 3:19; Galatians 3:19–26).

43. Read Psalm 119:73 and Luke 12:7, 22–34. What do these passages teach about the relationship between God and us? Why should we trust God's Word to be authoritative even over the dreams we have?

The fact that dreams have different possible causes or sources should also tell us of the danger in relying upon them for guidance. Dreams could come from God or from our own "mental downloading" of experiences or images. Because of the possibility of different causes for dreams, we are already left on shaky grounds for trusting them.

We see an immediate difference with regard to God and His Word. God is the one ultimate cause for genuine revelation, and such revelation is found in Holy Scripture. God may have used men to write what He has revealed, but such revelation is ultimately grounded in Him (2 Peter 1:20–21). Therefore, when we rely on Scripture, we are not relying on shaky grounds because we have the assurance that it comes from one source, namely God.

Real Redemption

What we dream does not create or destroy what is real. I can remember having a dream in which I was Spider-Man. But I did not wake up in a red and blue suit with the ability to fire webs at criminals or at my coffee maker to pull in a morning cup of joe.

It may seem silly for me to state that dreams are not real. But a philosophical belief known as *solipsism* makes this necessary.

Solipsism teaches that there is no reality existing outside of the mind. Under this theory the world is basically an illusion, a vast dreamland.

Although Walsh proposes that dreams may act as "incarnations" of truth, they do not offer what the Incarnate One—Jesus Christ—offers, namely real forgiveness and eternal life.

Some modern theologians treat Christianity as an ideal. They describe Christ as a creation of the disciples to embody that ideal. But Christ is more than an ideal Savior. He is not a fictional character dreamt up by human imagination. Rather He is a historical being who really dwelt among men (John 1:1–14).

Why does this matter? Scripture tells us that "without the shedding of blood there is no forgiveness" (Hebrews 9:22). Since Scripture also tells us that the Law holds us condemned, we need the forgiveness of sins. We need a physical and real being to shed blood for forgiveness. As both God and man, Christ provides what is necessary for salvation: shedding His blood as a *man*, and applying it with infinite forgiveness as *God*.

44. Read Hebrews 9:11–22; Isaiah 43:11; Mark 2:5–7. What do these passages tell us about the necessity of a savior being both God and man?

Some regard the idea of heaven and eternal peace as mere dreams, a form of escapism from suffering, a destitute life, and depression. Christ does not promise that our relationship will be void of all suffering, but He gives us joy in the midst of suffering (John 15:11). Moreover, the suffering you may experience as a Christian does not compare to the promise and glory of eternal life (Romans 8:18). You will experience the struggles of the sinful flesh and persecution for following Christ, but Christ has given you His love and the Holy Spirit to help you through the troubles of this present world (Romans 8:26–28). Furthermore, Christ has promised to bear your burdens, and He admonishes you to cast them upon Himself (Matthew 11:28–30).

God, in Christ, forgives you all your sins (1 John 1:9). Assurance no longer is to be found in dreams, but rather in God's promises through Jesus Christ. Rather than having assurance in the "incarnational" symbols of dreams, you have assurance in the Incarnate One, Jesus Christ. You have assurance in Christ because He is the Truth. This means He not only communicates truth, but also has fulfilled what He set out to do: to die as a ransom for you and to rise again for your justification (Mark 10:45; Romans 3:22–25; 1 Peter 1:21)! Our dreams do not have the creative power of Christ. He is living and active today, providing a sure and strong foundation for you through His Word.

Words
to Remember

We demolish arguments and every pretension that sets itself up against the knowledge of God, and we take captive every thought to make it obedient to Christ. 2 Corinthians 10:5

CHAPTER FIVE

Demons

Williiam Peter Blatty's novel of a young girl possessed by the devil, The *Exorcist*, remains one of the most chilling and horrifying stories ever made into a film. During the early stages of her possession, the girl, Regan, exhibits unusual behavior, such as superhuman strength, different personalities, and blasphemous language. The mother of the young girl takes her to a series of doctors. But, after being examined by a host of doctors and psychologists, no natural explanation is found for Regan's condition. The doctors then suggest that the mother contact a witch doctor or someone with expertise in delivering spirits.

Eventually, the mother contacts Father Karras, a Jesuit priest who does not believe in the possibility of possession. (The priest was taught by modern theology and psychology that demonic possession does not occur.) After he visits the possessed girl, he seeks permission from his bishop to conduct an exorcism as a type of placebo, the idea being that a ceremony could ease the psychological pain Regan was struggling with. The bishop assigns another priest experienced in exorcism for assistance. Both priests engage in a vehement spiritual battle with the devil using the rite of exorcism as found in the *Rituale Romanum*.

45. Do you think that demons could really possess both the body and the soul of a human individual? Why or why not?

William Peter Blatty's novel is loosely based on a true story. Blatty based his story on the 1949 case of a twelve-year-old boy from Maryland. The boy was brought to St. Louis, MO, after the spontaneous etching of "Louis" appeared on his abdominal region. Since his parents were Lutherans, they sought help from a Lutheran seminary. When the Lutheran ministers failed to help the boy, the parents took him to some local Jesuits, who performed an exorcism.

46. Read 2 Peter 2:4; Jude 6; Mark 1:23–26; 5:1–15. What do these verses tell you about the nature and state of fallen angels, otherwise known as demons?

Demonic Influence

Many people today dismiss the existence of the devil and demons. They reason that since demons are not physical beings, no one can prove their existence. Therefore they must not exist.

It is also very common for people to dismiss the existence of demons in the same way the priest dismissed them in *The Exorcist*. That is, people often think that demonic intervention was an idea left back in the 1500s or earlier, that people of old who believed in demonic intervention, were superstitious and lacked the tools of science or psychology to understand mental illness. They trust that our modern psychology explains away so-called demonic possession.

47. Can psychology offer a comprehensive explanation for demonic intervention? Why or why not?

In his book, *The House Swept Clean*, Darrell McCulley suggests different ways in which demonic intervention can occur. He argues that demonic intervention does not necessarily mean full bodily possession, as in the 1949 exorcism case. There are other ways in which demons manifest themselves. Demonic activity is also found in the following: (1) miraculous healing, (2) "parlor tricks," and (3) direct communication. We will examine these categories one at a time.

Many people report that they have experienced miraculous healing through a spiritual medium. Such mediums may treat people with elixirs or other mysterious potions. McCulley suggests that such reports may be based on demonic activities.

One may wonder why a demon would *heal* someone. McCulley points out that demons can do such things to create credibility in a medium. If a medium heals someone of a disease, people may put their trust in the medium rather than in Christ. In this way, people are directed away from Christ, which was the ultimate goal of the demon working through the medium.

48. Read 2 Thessalonians 2:9–12. What things will Satan use in an attempt to deceive us?

"Parlor tricks" refers to levitating objects, mysterious noises, apparitions, or objects moving without any apparent physical cause. People generally believe that such things happen because of a disembodied spirit (ghost). But Job tells us that the dead do not come back (Job 7:9–10).

49. In light of Job 7:9–10 and Hebrews 9:27, what do you think about the common hauntings and ghost stories people often tell?

Finally, demons also intervene through *direct communication* to mediums. Unlike "parlor tricks," this method goes beyond bodily manifestations to the point of relaying information. As mentioned above, the dead simply do not come back. But, demons may relay false information to psychics and mediums as a way of undercutting something directly asserted in God's Word. Think about the impact such misleading information could have. If a demon relays information to a medium who thinks they have actually contacted a dead spirit, they could convince the medium and others that not only are the dead able to communicate from "beyond" but also that eternal bliss with Christ is unnecessary.

50. Read Acts 16:16–18; 19:13–20. What connection do you see here between demons and practices such as divination and magic arts?

God
Warns Us

S cripture does not explicitly tell us how demons possess an individual or why they inflict people with particular torments. However, God's Law clearly commands us to turn away from any form of divination (Deuteronomy 18:10–12). That is, we are forbidden to attempt contacting the dead through spiritists or psychic mediums.

Despite this clear warning from God's Word, popular culture encourages people to dabble in the spirit world. For example, ouija boards are another form of divination. It is amazing how ouija boards, things that appear so harmless that they are sold in toy stores (and made by Parker Brothers!), are actually spiritually destructive. It should be noted that the boy possessed in the true-life exorcism story (pp. 37–38) used forms of divination, including a ouija board. (Evidently, the ouija board was one of his direct avenues to the demonic.)

51. Read Deuteronomy 18:10–12. With today's fascination for the supernatural, how should we as Christians warn others of the dangers connected with divination?

Another example of the effects of divination is found in an event involving two young women over twenty years ago. Gerald Brittle's book, *The Demonologist*, records the account of two roommates who used a ouija board and contacted what they thought was the spirit of a young girl named Annabelle. This spirit wanted to be brought back to this world for the purpose of finding "peace." Feeling sorry for the spirit, the women continued to contact it through the ouija board. This led to a series of mysterious and terrifying events including the possession and movement of a doll, the appearance of written messages, and an attack on the fiancé of one of the women. The women then sought help, contacting professional demonologists, Ed and Lorraine Warren, who performed an exorcism.

52. Read Acts 19:13–16. How might a rite for exorcism be helpful?

Idolatry is another avenue for demons. Demons can intervene in this world through just about anything one sets up as an idol. Darrell McCulley reported to me the experience of a high school friend who set up a sculpture in his room as an idol. McCulley's friend gave the sculpture a name and talked to it much like one would a pet. Then, his sculpture started appearing in different places in the room even though his friend had not moved it. Suspicious of his own memory, one night the young man made sure to set the sculpture in one distinct position. When it appeared in a completely different place, he began to worry.

53. Read Matthew 4:8–10; Isaiah 14:12–15. What can you gather from these texts about the character of the devil? What is the Christian response to demonic idolatry?

Christic
the Victor

54. Read about the Gerasene demoniac in Mark 5:1–20 and Luke 8:27–39. Discuss whether a Christian can become demon-possessed.

The belief that Christians may be demon-possessed may come from experiences people have had with divination. For example, if Christians use such things as the ouija board, then it seems that they, too, could become possessed.

It is important to distinguish between sins done *in* faith and losing one's faith. The former regards the sins committed against God's commandments. Practicing divination is not an unforgivable sin. A doubting or confused Christian may partake in divination out of ignorance. That does not mean that person has denied his or her faith or become demon-possessed.

55. Read Acts 26:17–18; Colossians 1:13; Ephesians 2:1–7; Luke 22:31–32. What do these verses tell us about our salvation in Christ and His protection?

Faith grafts you into Christ. You are under His Lordship. You are sons/daughters of God through faith and Holy Baptism (Galatians 3:26–27). As Luther's *Small Catechism* states, Baptism "works forgiveness of sins, [and] rescues [us] from death and the devil." Likewise, the Holy Spirit is given as a deposit to you, the believer. Both your body and spirit belong to God through Christ's blood (1 Corinthians 6:19–20). Since you belong to Christ by faith, you are also a bearer of His name.

The name of Christ has tremendous power! It is the very name at which every knee should bow when He returns in glory (Philippians 2:10). As bearers of Christ's name, we have His authority, and this includes authority over the evil one.

56. Read Mark 3:13–15, 23–30; Luke 10:18–20; 1 John 4:4; James 4:7; 1 Corinthians 6:3; 2 Peter 2:4. What do these passages tell you about the standing that both Christ and Christians have towards demons?

The evidence of Scripture about Christ's and the Christians' authority over the devil and demons is that they cannot threaten Christ's people. Moreover, Matthew 26:53 tells us about Christ's authority over good angels. If good and upright angels serve Christ, how could even a multitude of *fallen* angels stand up to Him! Even the devil needs Christ's permission to test one of His saints (Luke 22:31–32).

Words
to Remember

In all these things we are more than conquerors through Him who loved us. Romans 8:37

CHAPTER SIX

Angels

A loud thunderclap sounds. A heavenly manifestation unfolds. Before a multitude of priests, an image suddenly appears at the altar of the church. The image brightly illuminates the altar in a supernatural spectacle. An angelic apparition appears before their very eyes! The angel is judged to be Michael, the angel of justice and the avenger of evil.

A group of people attending service at St. Francis Xavier Church in St. Louis described this event in 1949. They explained that this vision of an angel appeared at about the same time that the boy from the exorcist story was delivered from demonic possession (pp. 37–38). The priests who witnessed the apparition thought the angel's appearance was a sign of God's victory.

57. Every year Christians claim to receive visits from angels. What do you think of such angel stories?

58. In what ways have you seen the general culture (including television shows, films, art, etc.) depict angels?

Science and Angels

A ngels are definitely not something you see everyday. Since science primarily investigates material causes or tangible realities, it does not seem possible for scientists to investigate angelic beings. Angels cannot be placed under a microscope like an amoeba or an insect. Angelic beings are "heavenly beings" and spiritual. It is important to remember, however, that there are many examples in Scripture where angels were observable.

59. Read Genesis 19:1–13 and Isaiah 6:1–7. Summarize how these passages depict angels.

Subjects for scientific investigation are usually observed repeatedly (such as the sun rising or snow falling.) But angels don't appear in a regular way.

However, the *quality* of an observance, rather than *quantity*, can help validate our knowledge of something's existence. For example, astronauts who observed the round shape of the earth from outer space for the first time made such a quality observance of the planet. The earth stood before them in its mass and shape so convincingly, that they did not need a series of tests to validate whether it was really round or not.

We often doubt things that are not readily available to the senses. Accounts of angelic appearances are often personal. For example, Isaiah seemed to be the sole witness of the angels who appeared to him. And Joseph and Mary were visited individually by angels (Matthew 1:20; Luke 1:30–35).

60. How can we have any certainty for the existence of angels?

The account of the angel appearing at the church in St. Louis has some credibility. After all, a number of people testified about what they saw. It is hard to dismiss the event as a hallucination or mere "dreaming" because more than one person claimed to have observed the angel. At the same time, one should not make belief in such an event a basis for the Christian faith or a point of obsession. The Lord's angels serve the Lord and want us to focus on Him.

The Lord's Messengers

People today seek hope. But often they seek hope from sources other than the Lord. Even angels can become inappropriate objects of hope. Two world-views influence our sense of hope: naturalism (belief in only the material or physical) and supernaturalism (focus on the heavenly and immaterial). We live in an age of paradox. Some people are apt to dismiss the reality of things unseen, while others focus almost completely on the supernatural.

61. Read Matthew 4:1–11 and Luke 1:30–38. What do we find as the primary role of angels in these verses?

The First Commandment expressly forbids man to set up anything as an object of worship in place of God (Exodus 20:3). If we look for salvation from something other than the Savior, Jesus Christ, we are also guilty of idolatry and unbelief. Angels are not our *saviors*, they are our *servants*. They do not do anything apart from God's command on our behalf. God is the ultimate cause for their protection over us, thus we can thank God for angelic protection.

62. Read Psalm 91:9–13 and Hebrews 1. How do these passages describe the interaction between God, angels, and humans?

Psalm 8:5 tells us that God made humankind "a little lower than the heavenly beings." Because of our natural propensity towards idolatry, we will even make an object of worship out of something that is at a lower status than God. Although angels are truly magnificently created beings and possess far greater power than ourselves, they are still less in power and authority than God.

63. Read Psalm 8. What does this chapter tell us about God's relationship to what He has created (including angels)?

If an angel appears to us in a dream or in any other manner, we should not be so quick to assume that it is directly from God. We are called to test the spirits and to see whether they are from God (1 John 4:1).

In case of such an event, one should "catechize the spirit." This does not mean you play Bible Trivia. Even false spirits may come across as well instructed in the faith. Instead, request that the spirit confess Christ as its Lord. Only by the Holy Spirit can a person confess that Christ is Lord (1 Corinthians 12:3), so simply ask the spirit who is its Master or Lord. If the spirit can confess Christ as Lord, then it is sent from God. But, if the spirit is unwilling, or evades the question, then it is a false spirit, and a messenger of Satan. You must always remember that even the devil can disguise himself as an angel of light (2 Corinthians 11:14).

64. What do you think of testing the spirits? Is the question of Lordship a valid criterion for establishing the truthfulness of a spirit?

Angels Are Servants of the Good News

We may regard the protection God provides through angels as one of the blessings of the Gospel. Although they did not purchase eternal life for us as did Christ, nonetheless, they are sent to care for us (Acts 27:23; Psalm 34:7; 91:9–13; Hebrews 1:14).

The concept of a *personal* guardian angel is alluded to in Scripture but is not emphasized (Matthew 18:10; Acts 12:15). Scripture emphasizes a general protection of angels over the saints, instead of a "Clarence" (the guardian angel for Jimmy Stewart's character in the film *It's a Wonderful Life*). Additionally, Scripture does not teach that people become angels when they die.

65. The concept of a personal guardian angel may provide us comfort, but how might emphasis on such an idea confuse people?

There is much superstition regarding the person and work of angels. During medieval times, people generally held to such high supernaturalistic views that they tended to perceive a spirit "behind every bush." Today, we may often find people believing that angels come to comfort people in a random manner. Angels tend to be viewed as divine "pillow-fluffers" that help us in every little discomfort we experience.

66. Read Isaiah 37:36 and Joshua 5:13–15. How does this verse present a different view of angels?

Scripture does not tell us that angelic protection is random. There seems to be a definite and set purpose as to the nature of their protection. Since angels work according to God's purpose and at His command, we can only conclude that there is a definite and organized principle behind it. Although how angels work may be mysterious to us, we can be assured that their purpose is for the glory of God. God does not do things chaotically or randomly, but carries out His plan to His glory while working all things in conformity with His will (Ephesians 1:11).

Angels serve God by serving His plan of salvation in the Gospel. For example, the angel Gabriel announced to Mary that she was going to bear the Son of God (Luke 1:26–31). Likewise, we also see a similar event in the case of Samson's birth (Judges 13:1–5). Angels are servants to Christ and act on Christ's command (Matthew 26:53). Since they have a subordinate role to Christ and His will, we can have confidence that angels will be there for our good.

67. Read Colossians 2:18–19. What kind of things does the Word tell us to watch out for and implicitly warn us against?

In spite of our idolatry or trust in things other than God, Christ forgives our sin. Angels point you to the Savior who removes your guilt. They are God's messengers who serve the most important message—salvation wrought through the death and resurrection of Christ. Angels are always there for you because you belong to Christ.

We should remember that our one true security is offered us in the blood of Christ. We contact this source of true security in the Word and the Sacraments. Tangible things give certainty, and such tangible realities can be found in the preached word of Christ's forgiveness, the certainty of your bond with God through Baptism, and participation "in" the body and blood of Christ at the Lord's Table.

If you feel the need to find security in angels, recall that even angels worship the Son of God. Moreover, angels would not exist if Christ had not created them in the first place. Therefore, Christ alone is your hope and trust who bought you with His own blood (Hebrews 1:3–6; 9:11–22; 10:10, 19).

Words
to Remember

For He will command His angels concerning you to guard you in all your ways; they will lift you up in their hands, so that you will not strike your foot against a stone. Psalm 91:11–12

Leader Notes

Leaders, this guide is provided as a "safety net," a place to turn for help in answering questions and for enriching discussions. It will not answer every question raised in your class. Please read it along with the questions before class. Consult in class only after exploring the Bible references and discussing what they teach.

Please note the different abilities of your class members. Some will easily find Bible passages and pronounce the terms used in this study. Others will struggle. To make participation easier, team up members of the class. For example, if a question asks you to look up several passages, assign one passage to one group, the second to another, and so on. Divide up the work! Let participants present the different answers that they discover. Also, have participants turn to the glossary at the back of this book for help with technical terms.

Each topic is divided into four sections:

Focus introduces the topic for discussion.

Science critique summarizes what modern science has discovered about the topic.

Law critique considers the topic in view of God's commands.

Gospel affirmation helps participants understand how God addresses the issues raised by the topic through His Son, Jesus Christ.

CHAPTER ONE

Miracles

Objectives

By the power of the Holy Spirit working through God's Word, participants will have a better understanding of the relationship between science and miracles; learn criteria for discerning between true and false miracles; and learn that miracles done by God have a unique and set purpose.

1. Answers will vary. Some may not have experienced such an event. The point here is not to figure out who has the best miracle story, but to open a discussion of the relationship between miracles and God's purpose behind them.

2. God is not a "cosmic-magician." God does not do powerful and wondrous things for mere shock value. Apologist Paul Little affirmed that God's miraculous works were not done to simply astound people and mesmerize them. They had a broader purpose behind them, namely, the salvation of souls. When a remarkable thing occurs for human benefit (such as the one that occurred for the men in the Harkness) it may very well be from God, and it may very well not be. If there had been no salvific goal in the act of the miracle, then it is possible that it is not from God. God wants people to receive the spiritual benefits of Christ.

3. Answers will vary. Explore the difficulties of easily or quickly attributing something to God's will.

4. The story of Lazarus in John 11 addresses the problem of evil and how God relates to the world. Note how Jesus said that Lazarus's illness would not lead to death (v. 4). Yet, later, Jesus stated that Lazarus had died (v. 14). Jesus speaks with *equivocation*. He uses the

same word (death) in different senses or meanings. In verse 4, Jesus is saying that Lazarus will not die in an ultimate sense or he will not remain dead. In verse 11, Jesus refers to death in the temporal sense as one's ceasing to exist in this life (also vv. 25–26).

The story of Lazarus shows that eternal, spiritual needs take precedence over temporal, physical needs. Jesus gave faith priority over healing an illness. What happens in this life is subordinate to the promises given in Christ through faith. Christ times the whole situation in order to lead people to a greater good—faith in Him (vv. 4, 14, 42–45; John 14:11).

It should also be noted that even though Christ did not prevent Lazarus's death, He did not cause it. Humanity brought death upon itself through the disobedience in the garden of Eden (Romans 5:12–14; 1 Corinthians 15:22).

Doubts about Miracles

5. Answers will vary. A miracle stands outside the normal course of natural law. Science is useful for considering any event, but cannot prove the existence of miracles. Among other reasons, this is because our experiences with our senses are very limited. We are often poorly prepared to judge the experiences of others. (You may have heard someone say, "If I can't see it, I won't believe it!")

By their very definition, miracles defy explanation. In his book, *Know Why You Believe,* Paul Little discusses the ongoing debate about the very nature and definition of miracles. Some say that they act *against* the normal course of nature while others believe that they are *outside* of it. It may be noted that God is the Creator of the world and is therefore the Author and Sustainer of natural laws. So no matter how one defines miracles, there is a fundamental agreement that God can do what He wills with regard to the natural laws of the world—He is not subject or bound to them. Christ demonstrated His authority over nature (Mark 4:35–41; 6:45–52; John 2:5–11).

6. Science presents us with a set of observable facts, things that can be seen, demonstrated, and repeated. But we must remember that something's existence is not dependent upon whether we have observed it or not.

7. The passages present God as the mighty creator, judge, and sustainer of all things that exist. He maintains His care and concern for all living creatures. He is perfectly capable of doing miracles. Jesus' words emphasize that God is our *Father*. But He has purpose in His actions: to care for us and call us back to Himself (Mark 10:27; Romans 11:33–36).

Miracles and Manipulation

8. God tells the Israelites to rely on what is revealed to them in His Word. To go beyond the Lord's self-revelation is not only going beyond God's will, but also going against it. Furthermore, it is a fruitless endeavor. Speculation is just that: speculation. How can somebody know what is not available to them for examination? Emphasize that what God has revealed to us in His Word is sufficient for our knowledge concerning Him and our salvation.

9. Job tells us that God does things that we cannot comprehend. We need faith as well as reason. Even though God does things that are beyond our reason, it does not mean that He does things that are *irrational*. They stand beyond the *capacity* for human reason but not *against* it. Faith is God's gift for apprehending those things which we cannot grasp by our reason (Hebrews 11:1).

10. Speculating about things God has not revealed can be fruitless. If we have a minimal understanding of what is revealed, how much less will we understand what is not revealed?

11. Answers may vary. A miracle does not validate the person who performs it.

12. Matthew 4:1–11 shows us that even Satan can use Scripture. He may also use miracles or remarkable events for his own damnable purpose: to lead people away from Christ. The Gospel provides the surest grounds for testing deeds and claims. God came in the flesh to redeem mankind from their sins and save them through faith in Christ alone. See Galatians 1:8; 1 John 4:1–4; John 8:44; 2 Timothy 2:24–26; 1 Peter 5:8; Luke 22:31–32.

The Lord
of Miracles

13. Answers will vary. Encourage participants to share their thoughts about the miracle of Easter. Note what people base their faith on. Is there a subjective basis (personal experience/feelings) or an objective basis (facts, events, persons, etc.)? Apologist Paul Little once said that whenever he had serious doubts with regard to his faith, he always went back to two things: (1) the objective historical facts pertaining to Christ, and (2) the subjective experience of how Christianity changed his life. Both are important. But the objective basis of our faith has more solid ground because it is not dependent upon our ever-changing emotions or personal experiences.

14. The resurrection is central to our faith! The resurrection separates the Christian faith from all other religions. The ability to raise a person from the dead is a power unique to God. Scripture denotes that only God has the power to resurrect people from the dead (Psalm 68:20; Revelation 1:18; 2 Kings 5:7). The resurrection of Christ bears witness to the fact that He is God (John 2:19–22)!

15. The resurrection is not only central to our faith in the objective sense, but also in the subjective sense. Luther wrote that the Christian undergoes a "daily Baptism." Luther meant that the Christian needs to repent and "drown" the old Adam daily, putting to death the sinful nature. We daily participate in Christ's death and resurrection by being raised in newness of life through the power of the Holy Spirit (Colossians 3:5–10; Galatians 5:22–26). And, if the resurrection of Christ had not occurred, this subjective resurrection would have no basis. Our spiritual resurrection presupposes the victory over death won by Christ. In our "daily Baptism," we participate in a death and resurrection because of the death and resurrection of Christ (Romans 6:1–11)!

CHAPTER TWO

Mystical Experiences

Objectives

B y the power of the Holy Spirit working through God's Word, participants will learn about the nature of mystical experience; understand abuses of mysticism in deviating from the mediatory role of the Word and Sacraments; gain a healthy respect for both reason and faith; and review experiences in view of God's Word.

16. There may be several answers to this question since mysticism takes on different faces. Although the term is not used very often in everyday conversation, mysticism can be found in New Age practice and belief as well as in the religions of Buddhism, Islam, and even Christianity. Additionally, practices that are clearly mystical may have quasi-scientific names, such as "Transcendental Meditation."

The Greek term *mysterion* means "something that closes the mouth," In other words, an act that makes someone speechless with amazement or causes them to keep a secret. Mysticism appears in all world religions, and has a common goal: to engage the divine without the use of reason but through direct experience.

17. St. Paul's experience may seem very much like that of St. Francis. They both received direct revelations of Jesus Christ. Yet St. Paul's experience also differs from St. Francis's experience. First, Paul's experience had witnesses who observed the light that confounded and blinded St. Paul (Acts 22:9). The earliest recorded statement for St. Francis's experience dates a century after the alleged event. Second, St. Francis's experience followed an extreme fast and extended meditation, two conditions known to bring on delirium. Acts

does not record that St. Paul was fasting or meditating prior to his encounter with Christ on the Damascus road. He began a journey from Jerusalem (where the high priest was) to Damascus (about a 150 miles) with the intent of arresting Christians (9:1–2). Moreover, the narrative states that St. Paul fasted *after* the encounter with Christ, and not *before* (v. 9). Someone may argue that St. Paul was in an unusual or guilt-ridden state of mind because of his murderous attitude towards Christians, but that does not necessarily mean that he suffered from hallucinations of any sort. His intense persecution of Christians was motivated by his zeal for the Law (Galatians 1:13–14).

Evaluating Experiences

18. Answers may vary. It is fairly common today for people to claim that Jesus appeared to them in a vision or dream. Some charismatic Christians claim to have had private revelations of Christ prior to their conversion or after their conversion.

19. First, Christ suffered to take away our sins, not to gain some personal spiritual experience. Genuine suffering, by nature, is something that *happens* to an individual, not something an individual seeks in order to earn a spiritual badge. Thus, suffering is *passive* and not *active*. Scripture never commands us to seek out suffering.

Also, Scripture never promises that we will live totally without suffering as Christians. Scripture offers encouragement and precepts on how to deal with suffering by pointing to Christ as our example of patient endurance. Scripture consistently describes suffering as a result of persecution, not something a person should impose upon themselves.

20. Love for Christ and keeping His Word go hand-in-hand. If we truly love Christ, we will keep His Word and see it as sufficient enough for maintaining a proper understanding of His work on the cross. Both Word and Sacrament are presented in Scripture as means connecting us to Christ and His death on the cross. They connect us in both the remembrance and in the reception of His benefits—the forgiveness of our sins merited by His death. Therefore, one who seeks to know Christ and His cross apart from Word and Sacrament is not motivated by a love for Christ, but rather by something else—likely, spiritual pride or vain sentimentality.

God Works
through Means

21. They heard the voice of the LORD. Also, the expression translated for "cool of the day" uses *ruach*, the Hebrew word for "wind." In other words, God made Himself present through a physical reality—a breeze of wind. Luther notes in his commentary on Genesis how this manifestation of God occurs as a result of sin. That is, because of sin, humans can no longer be in God's presence apart from mediation.

Mediatory forms hide the fullness of God's glory and therefore provide a way for man to approach God safely. For man to have direct contact with God would result in death (Exodus 33:20). Prior to the fall, man dwelt with God in an immediate way, when Adam and Eve were without sin. Likewise, St. John describes how after Christ returns "we shall see Him as He is" (1 John 3:2), which happens at our glorification when our sinfulness will be eradicated. Also note the apparent contradiction with regard to this view in light of Exodus 33:11. If you pair it up with verse 20 you will see the distinction. Verse 11 does not deal with the *mode of God's presence* in the act of speaking with Moses, but rather portrays an image of how God will relate to His people. The same concept here could be applied to the incident of the burning bush in Exodus 3. God conversed with Moses without any agents or messengers to communicate what God wanted to say, however, the way in which God communicated to Moses was directly person-to-person through a burning bush. Verse 20 regards the mode of God's presence. No one shall see His being as it is or in a direct, unmediated way. Such a thing is dangerous because man cannot handle the magnitude of God's presence unfiltered by physical means.

22. The words of Christ are not mere text, they are spiritual words (John 6:63). The Words of Scripture present God's very Spirit to us. God speaks to us, revealing His character and salvation.

Furthermore, the Sacraments provide us with God's presence because His Spirit is present in Baptism (1 Corinthians 6:11; Colossians 2:11–12) and Christ's body and blood are present in the Lord's Supper (Mark 14:22–24).

23. Luther's exposition on the Lord's Prayer in the Small Catechism provides a great resource for understanding the nature and

purpose of prayer. Note that prayer is, indeed, relational by nature. That is, it involves man offering up petitions and supplications towards God. But, in this relational action between man and God, one is not called to ascend and lose oneself in God through mystical experience. (Prayer depends on the Word of God.)

God's Gracious Gifts Found through Means

24. Answers will vary. The question probes the strength of the participants' faith in Christ. Remember that it is not the degree of faith that saves, but rather it is faith *alone* that brings a person into salvation (John 6:29; Mark 9:24). In this life, our faith will never be totally perfect. Encourage participants to abide in the True Vine. This is done by continually partaking of Christ's Word and Sacrament (John 15:1–8).

25. The Gospel motivates us to trust God because it declares the love of God for us! Note that what reminds us of God's love for us is the cross and the things that link us to the cross—the Word, Baptism, and the Lord's Supper.

CHAPTER THREE

Near-Death Experiences

Objectives

By the power of the Holy Spirit working through God's Word, participants will learn about near-death experiences and consider their truthfulness; understand them in light of Scripture; have confidence in Christ as the Lord of the living and the dead; and understand the role and significance of the death and resurrection of Christ for their personal lives.

26. People may be reluctant to share personal near-death experience. The point of the question is to open a discussion about the claims that are out there and the research being done on them.

Modern Research

27. Answers will vary. Both nihilism and naturalism contain unwarranted philosophical claims and do not sufficiently explain away near-death experiences.

28. Fundamentally, it is difficult to answer absolutely because the nature of such events lie outside the realm of science. Near-death experiences are extremely subjective. They can only be observed by an individual. In a sense, this phenomenon is one of those "I won't

know until I see it for myself" things. However, we should assess the evidence available to us and examine it in light of Scripture.

29. Moody's explanations are fairly well thought out, yet uncertainty remains. Human experience and scientific proposals offer insufficient help for evaluating such experiences. We need the certain testimony of God's Word.

Death as a Result of the Fall

30. These verses describe the separation of body and soul at the time of death. The "earthly tent" refers to the mortal body. The "heavenly dwelling" refers to the glorified body we will receive at the time of the resurrection at the Last Day. St. Paul teaches that to be at home in the body is to be away from Christ. But, to be apart from the body, is to be in Christ's presence. One does not merely cease to exist as nihilism teaches.

31. Some ask, "Why should I be responsible for what one man did thousands of years ago?" God created Adam and Eve and gave them a free choice affecting the rest of the human race. It is important to note that Adam was not simply one individual, but a human being comprising all humanity. The Hebrew term *adam* means "humankind." Adam comprised all humanity in himself and therefore we all participated in the fall.

32. The nature of Stephen's testimony is mysterious. It is important to note how he described seeing Christ before the stoning started. Hence, it is not a near-death experience. Note Stephen's prayer and how Jesus, who is "seated at the right hand of the heavenly Father," stands to welcome Stephen.

33. The Scripture describes people's souls as conscious or aware after death. *Sleep* in the New Testament, when describing death, is a euphemism that describes our rest in Christ. (Hebrews 4:9–11; Revelation 14:13)

Christ the Lord
of Life and Death

34. Note that these verses show us the willingness of Christ to suffer on our behalf. The Corinthians passage associates death and life with two different ministries: that of Moses and that of Christ. Christ brought what Moses' ministry could not bring—life and glory. Death is confirmed in Moses' ministry, whereas it is annulled in Christ's ministry.

35. Before justification the "old self" cannot possibly please God. By participating in Jesus' death through our Baptism, the old self is put to death. After justification the new self lives the sanctified life by the working of the Holy Spirit (1 Corinthians 6:9–11). See also 2 Corinthians 4:7–18; Colossians 3:1–17; and 1 John 2:1. Therefore, the death and resurrection of Christ accomplish not only the justification of the Christian, but also the sanctification.

CHAPTER FOUR

Dreams

Objectives

By the power of the Holy Spirit working through God's Word, participants will learn about dreams and their interpretation in the Bible; evaluate popular and scientific ideas about dreams; and celebrate the reality and comfort of God's revelation in Christ.

36. Answers may vary. Not everyone tells others about their dreams. Don't just gather anecdotal information about people's dreams. Discuss the nature of dreams and the comparison/contrast of our culture's perception of them and Joseph's brothers. Note where people are at with regard to dreams. Do they take them seriously or literally? Do they worry about their meaning?

Dreams and Their Interpretation

37. Make some important distinctions here. First, there is nothing we do or *can* do apart from God's omnipotence. Our very existence is grounded in His causal activity (Acts 17:24–28), and He provides for our physical and mental powers even when we use them for sinful acts. This does not mean that God works in us to commit sin or that He causes our dreams and nightmares. Theologian Thomas Aquinas made a helpful distinction between Primary and Secondary Causes. God is the Primary Cause of our existence, while the

Secondary Causes are a result of human actions—those actions, in turn, affect us individually as well as the world around us. In a similar manner, God can be seen as the Primary Cause for some dreams, but dreams are also a result of our own Secondary Causes. For example, worry can cause bad dreams and so can eating too much before going to bed. But dreams of all kinds appear to be a natural part of the R.E.M. stage of sleep and necessary for good mental health.

38. Answers will vary. Walsh is not saying that every dream is directly related to Christ. He asserts that Christ was the Incarnate Logos, or physical manifestation of God, He bridged the divine and the human by providing sensory imagery to man in communicating divine truth. In this sense, dreams act "incarnational" because they are symbolic realities of otherwise unknown meanings lying in the realm of sub-consciousness. Walsh's opinion may be interesting but needs to be tested against what Scripture teaches about dreams and Christ.

39. Allow participants to reflect on whether Walsh's theory on dreams fits with Scripture. On one hand, Walsh has a point in recognizing how dreams have a vital role with regard to revealing God's will. Scripture gives clear examples of God revealing His will to people in dreams. However, Walsh's evaluation of Joseph is highly unwarranted. There is simply no evidence that Joseph's dream manifested psychological issues. The text merely tells us that an angel came to him, and that Joseph feared for Mary's reputation because she was pregnant prior to their marriage (Matthew 1:19–20). Moreover, the text also tells us that Joseph was a just man, and not someone who was struggling for the ideal image of a hero. Conclusively, Walsh's interpretation "psychologizes" the text by reading modern ideas about dreams into the story.

40. Walsh's interpretation becomes man-centered because he speculates on the mind of Joseph. Walsh is discounting the truthfulness of Matthew's account by not letting it speak for itself. He subordinates the text to Jungian psychological theory. In other words, he is molding the text into his presupposed psychological theories. Dreams may truly have deep roots in the inner subconscious. But we cannot assert that *all* dreams are symbols of our innermost struggles or desires. Some dreams have their basis in God, as other biblical narratives point out (also Genesis 28:12–15).

41. Note that Joseph's dream involved an angel, but primarily an angel giving witness to and serving the Gospel of Christ. We should not be so apt to dismiss the reality of angels revealing themselves to

us. But, here is where the Gospel-principle (p. 6) comes into the picture again. We should measure dreams or visions in light of their relationship to the Gospel if we want to determine whether they are revealing God's will or not. For example, does the image point to objects of worship other than Christ? Does it motivate us to violate God's commands? Is it presenting a Christ other than the One found in Scripture? Is it somehow contradicting faith in Christ alone? Such questions are pertinent to the essence of the Gospel. As mentioned previously, the devil does not do things for the mere thrill of messing with people. The devil craftily does things to thwart people's salvation and obstruct them from the Gospel.

Empty Dreams

42. Note how the false prophets in Deuteronomy speak under an appealed authority to one of two names: (1) the name of the Lord or, (2) the name of their own god. God tells us that the false prophet speaks presumptuously when they claim to have received a direct revelation from Him, while not receiving His revelation at all. Also, note the value God places on dreams in contrast to His word (Jeremiah 23:28)!

43. God has created us and knows us better than we know ourselves. Here are two reasons to rely on God's Word above our own ideas or subjective emotions: (1) God is Creator and Sustainer of all things, and (2) God is omniscient. Since God has created all things, He knows the natural processes of our own lives as well as the world around us. Therefore, He has the authority to decide what is right and wrong. And, since God is also omniscient, it is only common sense to conclude that He knows what is best for us.

Trust in these truths comes from seeing God's goodness toward us. He is not totally transcendent to the point where He is uncaring for His creation, but rather, He provides for our every need and has reconciled us to Himself through Christ (2 Corinthians 5:19). Not many people will simply trust in the authority of a tyrant or an emotionless judge. But how many people have come to trust God's Word when they have seen that He became a man who sacrificed Himself and rose from the dead so that they, too, may escape death (Acts 2:36–41; 17:24–34)!

Real
Redemption

44. Essentially, these verses address both natures of Christ. Hebrews 9:22 shows that it is necessary for the shedding of blood to purchase forgiveness of sins. Since God is spirit (John 4:24), He is not made up of physical flesh and blood to purchase forgiveness—this is where the necessity of becoming man comes in. And since forgiveness of sins and eternal salvation could only be granted by God, it is necessary that God grant us such benefits. The effects of Christ's death carry benefits that only God could achieve. No man can give to God a ransom for another man (Psalm 49:7). Since only God has the power to forgive sins, and the blood of Christ forgives our sins, it follows that it is not the blood of a mere man, but the very blood of God Himself (1 John 1:7; Ephesians 1:7; Acts 20:28).

CHAPTER FIVE

Demons

Objectives

B y the power of the Holy Spirit working through God's Word, participants will learn about the possibility and manner of demonic intervention in the world; attain a biblical understanding of the nature of the devil and the demonic; and thank God for the authority they have over the devil and demons through Jesus Christ.

45. Identify where the participants are at with regard to the subject. Some Christians discount the possibility of demonic intervention in the world. But, if we truly take God's Word seriously, we should also take the possibility of demonic activity seriously (Ephesians 6:12). Moreover, the Lord would also have us take the ministry of Christ in this specific area seriously as well. For example, Mark 5:1–20 describes Jesus casting demons out of a man who was possessed.

46. These verses tell us that they are evil and act contrary to God and His will. Because of their rebellion against God, they have been reserved for judgment. That is why, in the Gospel accounts of Christ's encounter with them, they fear Christ's judgment. Christ possesses total authority over demons and they are afraid of Him. You will note in the Mark 5 account that there are a multitude of demons possessing the man. The demons' name, "Legion" may indicate that there were thousands of them since a Roman legion at that time consisted of thousands of soldiers.

Demons Influence

47. Psychology is the study of the human mind based on human behavior. Human behavior reveals what is going on in the mind. Since a psychologist learns about the mind through behavior, psychology has a basis as an empirical science.

Since demons are not physical beings, they lie outside of the range of the psychologist. But we should not disregard the use of psychology in interpreting whether someone is influenced by the demonic. Psychology helps us determine how the mind usually behaves (not everybody who acts unusual or speaks with different voices is demon-possessed). Moreover, not everyone who has been or can be demon-possessed is devoid of psychological illness. Darrell McCulley's book, *The House Swept Clean,* suggests that mental illness and possession may occur together in an individual. Ultimately, psychology may help us *discern* demonic influence in an individual, but not *determine* the demonic causes manifested in an individual.

48. The work of Satan through the man of lawlessness is two-fold: (1) to cause people to worship Satan, and (2) to deceive people so that they do not follow Christ. Satan wants to be higher than God and to be worshipped. Even when the devil tried to deceive Christ in the testing in the wilderness, he tried to get Christ to worship him (Matthew 4:9). He will use deception to lead souls astray from God. As long as someone does not believe in and obey Christ, they are carrying out Satan's will (John 8:41–44; Acts 26:17–18; Ephesians 2:2).

49. To put it plainly, the dead do not come back. This is disheartening to many because there are many people who want to contact their dead loved ones, either through an unexpected spiritual encounter or through a spiritist. Job 7:9–10 indicates that the dead do not return, but if there are further conflicts, demonstrate how when one dies, their soul is either: (1) with God in His kingdom, or (2) in hell (Philippians 1:23; 2 Corinthians 5:1–2; Luke 12:5; 16:19–31).

50. The texts show how spiritists and those who practice black magic tap into the demonic. These spirits could only be one of two things—either demons or spirits who have passed from this world into another. As shown above, souls of the dead have no contact with the living. Therefore, spirits involved in divination and the black arts are demons.

God
Warns Us

51. This is not an easy issue to deal with directly. If you know somebody involved with spiritism or any form of divination, it is imperative to warn them of the dangers. However, recognize that they may not listen to your concerns. People who practice such things are often prideful. The only way they can be delivered from such practices is through the power of God's Word and Spirit.

You may warn people directly with God's Law or point people to the love of Christ in His cross. Usually, the latter applies to people who are at some point of despair in their lives and need to hear a word of grace as opposed to Law.

I remember when I met a young man who claimed to follow Satan. He honestly believed that Satan was "on his side" and had more of a friendship role in his life. I explained to him that Satan hated him and that he only used people for his own purposes. I also explained to him that it was Satan's nature to lie. The young man seemed convinced and sat in shock and silence. Sadly, I never had the opportunity to speak with him again, but after the look on his face that evening, I would not be surprised if he gave up following Satan. The key to our discussion was helping him realize that Satan actually hated every ounce of him. Following this important point, I explained that Christ was His true friend. I communicated the Gospel to him. He appeared to give it serious consideration. Although he did not confess Christ as His Savior, the Word was sown in his heart so that it could sprout in God's time.

52. Many Christians have disdain for a formal rite of exorcism. They think that it is unnecessary or over ritualistic. (One example of rites for exorcisms can be found in the traditional *Rituale Romanum of 1614.* This service book uses many elaborate and superfluous wordings for the purpose of expelling a demon.) To some extent, such criticisms are warranted. However, Christians should not throw out the practice of exorcism, which is simply calling on God to remove the influence of the demonic. We should realize its proper form and place. For example, it used to be a common practice for Lutheran ministers to conduct an exorcism prior to Baptism (see *Lutheran Cyclopedia* pp. 287–88. Martin Luther rejected the medieval rite of exorcism because such rituals contained too many procedures and not

enough emphasis on the Word of God and prayer. Luther believed that all a Christian needed to do was pray over someone who was demon possessed to expel the demon. An exorcism liturgy could serve as a guideline for such prayer. One needs to know *what* to say in the prayer and *how* to say it. An exorcism rite would provide some of the necessary details for handling possessions. Perhaps the reason that the Lutheran minister involved with the 1949 exorcist story could not offer help was that he did not have a service for exorcism to guide him. He simply did not know what to do!

53. These texts describe the prideful character of the devil. The Isaiah text does not *directly* refer to the devil. It specifically describes the king of Babylon. However, interpreters have also viewed this passage as a comparison with the fall of Satan at the beginning of the world. (The Latin Vulgate uses "Lucifer" in v.12, which means "bearer of light" or "son of the dawn." Note how Jesus refers to this passage in Luke 10:17–18.) Satan was once the beautiful "son of the dawn." But he wanted to usurp God's majesty and be the highest being. The devil is swollen with pride up to this day and is on a vengeful mission to overthrow God's creation.

Christ rebuked the devil and quoted the passage from Deuteronomy (6:13) about how one is to serve and worship God alone. This reminds us to shun idolatry, seeking God and His kingdom as found in Jesus Christ.

Christ the Victor

54. Theologians have expressed different opinions on this issue. For example, Francis Pieper's *Christian Dogmatics vol. 1*, p. 509 states that Christians can become demon-possessed. The argument Pieper uses needs a serious reassessment since it robs the Christian of assurance that the Lord protects us from the evil one. He bases his statement on Mark 5:6, 18–19 and Luke 8:28, 38–39, the story of the Gerasenes demoniac. However, it is not at all clear that this man was a Christian or a Jewish believer. Other passages of Scripture emphasize the presence of the Holy Spirit in believers (e.g., Ephesians 1:13). Christians certainly struggle against Satan but remain the possession of God's Spirit (Romans 8:9–11, 38–39; Ephesians 6:10–18). The fol-

lowing questions and answers will explore this issue more thoroughly.

55. We are transferred from one dominion to another: the dominion of darkness and the devil to the dominion of Christ's kingdom. As Christians, we are under a new Lordship, that of Christ. Satan no longer has dominion over us, nor can he have dominion over us. Christ does not share His property. The devil has no rights over the Christian anymore because the Christian has been ransomed from his kingdom. Furthermore the examples of St. Peter and Job show how God protects His people from Satan (Luke 22:31; Job 1:9–12).

56. Demons are afraid of Christ! As inheritors of His kingdom we are given His rights and hold the power of His name. Luther mentioned in his treatise, *On the Freedom of a Christian*, how Christians are the bride of Christ and are given the full benefits and blessings of their groom. Demons are afraid of us because of the name we bear. Christians have been rescued from slavery to the devil and are no longer under his ownership. Christ's blood has ransomed you from the devil by bringing you safely into His glorious kingdom. Now, the devil and his minions are under God's authority!

Angels

Objectives

By the power of the Holy Spirit working through God's Word, participants will gain a biblical understanding of the nature of angels; recognize the possibility of angelic intervention in the world around us; and ask God to provide the protection of His angels.

57. Answers will vary. Angels remain a popular topic in our culture and, most recently, in television and movies. Many depictions of angels do not agree with biblical teaching. Participants should be prepared to change their attitudes and ideas about angels.

58. Share observations. The general culture has had a tremendous influence on people's attitudes and beliefs about the supernatural. Angels may be depicted as fat little babies on greeting cards or guardians/companions in TV shows and movies.

Science and Angels

59. Angels, although often described as "incorporeal" (having no physical body) appear to have taken physical form as described in the passage from Genesis. They not only appear in dreams (as one did for Joseph in Matthew 1:20) but also in history.

Isaiah describes the angels that surround God's throne. Multiwinged seraphs, they fly about serving the Almighty and praising Him with powerful voices.

60. Since most people do not see angels, they rely on the testi-

mony of those who have. The surest testimony on this topic comes from God's Word and not accounts from popular culture.

The Lord's Messengers

61. The role we find angels in here are as messengers and servants. Hence, they are subordinate to God, not only in their *being*, but also in their *role*. Angels are not equal to God, for they are created beings. They do not deserve worship. Although, God sends angels to our service, their service to us is ultimately founded on His decision. Hence, their service to us is their service to God. Psalm 91:11 tells us that it is God who gives His angels the charge of our protection.

62. The emphasis, here, is to show how it is God who sends angels. He is the One giving "charge" of His angels over the psalmist in this passage. This represents the reality of how angels receive their "orders" from God. They do not act in an autonomous way or choose to do as they please. Angels will not act apart from God's will or usurp their own desires above God's, otherwise they would fall into the same judgment as the *fallen* angels or demons (2 Peter 2:4, 11; Jude 6). Moreover, Hebrews 1 deals with the issue directly. We read in Hebrews 1:14, "Are not all angels ministering spirits sent to serve those who will inherit salvation?" The entire chapter of Hebrews 1 presents angels in a servant role both to Christ and the saints. Christ is clearly stated as having a superior office to the angels as they answer *to Him.*

63. This Psalm tells about God's majesty and authority over the world. While there is not a direct reference to God's status with regard to angels, we may infer that since God's glory exceeds over all His creation, angels, being created by God, are subordinate to His power and glory.

64. We should not go out on a witch hunt or actively engage in seeking the supernatural for the purpose of examination. Rather, when we are confronted by a spirit, or their doctrines, we are to test them to see if they are from God. In an audio lecture, the late apologist Walter Martin described an event in which a certain gentleman had a direct conversation with a spirit masquerading as his dead wife. The man thought that since his wife had died in Christ, she must have seen

Jesus. Before the man knew it was a false spirit, he asked it about Jesus. The spirit continued to evade the question. Perturbed, the man questioned the true identity of the spirit and pressed the question as to whether it could call Jesus "Lord" or not. The spirit wasted no time in retreating, being unwilling to answer the question.

Servants
of the Good News

65. Answers may vary. Out of his love for us in Christ, God truly sends angels to help His saints. Whether this help is in the form of a general blanket of assistance or a personal angel assigned to us, we cannot say. In either case, angels are not our spiritual "pets." They are mighty servants of our almighty Lord. One may certainly pray to God for the protection of His angels but one should not pray to or worship angels.

66. These verses simply denote how angels are not the soft and cuddly comforters that our culture so often depicts them to be. Scripture gives us a varied perspective of angels and their actions. God will use them to smite entire armies. In fact, you will note that in both passages, there was only *one* angel involved in inflicting violence upon the enemies of God's people. If only one angel can do this, imagine what several of them can do!

67. The apostle Paul warns us against false humility and the worship of angels. Christ is our Lord, but because of the old Adam within, we often diminish the Lordship of Christ in our own life.

It should be noted that it is not what we do with our life that makes Christ our Lord, but rather He is our Lord by faith through the power of the Holy Spirit (Romans 8:9–11, 1 Corinthians 6:19–20; 12:3). When we hold to Christ as the Substance and Center of our faith and life, we can place everything else subordinate to Him and His Lordship. We are free to serve Him and refrain from the captivity of idolatry which can even occur toward heavenly things such as angels.

The devil is so good at deceiving people that he would not mind for an instant if Christians were to worship the *good* angels. As long as people are worshipping something other than Christ, they are doing the devil's will.

Appendix

Science: Methods and Limits

At the foundation of modern science lies the scientific method. The scientific method lays ground rules for research and enables scientists to reliably discover the wonders of the universe. This in turn promotes greater learning for wider audiences. As technology advances and experiments continue to support scientific theories, writers report the findings, teachers educate their students, and knowledge of the universe increases. This in itself is wonderful!

A realistic and reasonable view of the methods and limits of science enables scientists as well as the general public to distinguish science fact from fiction. Science that is aware of its limits and proper methods in no way militates against religious faith. In fact, there are some similarities between scientific and theological methods.

What exactly is the scientific method, and why is it used? The scientific method establishes the foundation of scientific research. Simply put, it approaches knowledge of facts (science) in a systematic and experimental manner with logical steps. Following are the steps that help maintain the reliability of science:

Observations or measurements are made of the thing or event under investigation.

A hypothesis is proposed to explain observations.

The hypothesis helps to predict the results of new or additional observations.

The hypothesis is then tested against further observations or experiments and is modified if necessary to fit the new data. (It must fit the old data too!)

Steps three and four are repeated until the hypothesis no longer needs improvement. (Either it fits all the data and proves true, or one abandons the hypothesis.)

This simple explanation provides a rule for distinguishing *good* science from *bad* science. Fake observations can be uncovered if similar experiments by other scientists fail to produce the same results. Hence, good scientific method carries implications of honesty and integrity.

As useful as the scientific method is, it also has some important (and sometimes unappreciated) shortcomings, such as these:

The scientific method is better suited for methodical research than it is for unexpected discoveries. It implies systematic progress rather than a flash of inspiration from creativity.

The scientific method does not address unique events (events that cannot be reproduced), such as miracles or anomalies.

Even though the scientific method requires integrity, it cannot command it. Scientific hoaxes come and go. The existence of the scientific method does not mean that all scientists are honest. One can find hosts of Web sites and books devoted to describing hoaxes throughout the history of science.

The scientific method can become an excuse for elitism or resistance to new theories. In the past 50 years, plate tectonics went from a questioned theory to an accepted fact among geologists. Now that it is "fact," any theory that deviates from it meets the same kind of scorn that plate tectonics received only a few decades ago.

The scientific method can also become an excuse for avoiding issues. It is tempting to focus on research that explains *how* and to avoid questions of *why*. For example, physicists attempt to tell *how* the universe began but often skirt the issue of *why*.

As long as scientists follow the methods of science and recognize its unavoidable shortcomings, scientific and religious truths avoid conflict. Facts are facts, whether they are religious or scientific. However, a distinction must always be recognized between facts bound by time and space (scientific truths) and eternal, immutable facts (theological truths).

Glossary

autoscopic hallucinations. When one projects an image of themselves into visual space in a third-person perspective (e.g., meeting one's double on the street).

demonologist. Literally, "one who studies demons"; moreover, one who studies the nature and acts of demonic beings and other paranormal phenomena from a Christian perspective to help both Christians and non-Christians deal with their presence and occurrences in a healthy manner.

Gospel principle. Using the Gospel to discern the spiritual value of an event or teaching (see 1 John 4:1–3).

immediate revelation. The direct revelation of truth from God in the hearing or in the mind of an individual.

means. In theology, an object through which God reveals His teaching or blessing, such as the Bible, a Sacrament, a person, and so forth. The object stands as an intermediary for God's presence.

mediate revelation. See *means.*

metaphysics. Philosophical teaching that addresses the nature, origin, and understanding of reality.

naturalism. Philosophical worldview maintaining that nothing exists beyond the world of nature and material realities.

natural law. In science, the regular course of events occurring in nature at–large such as gravity, or energy loss in the atmosphere; description of events in the realm of nature that are seen as usually occurring as opposed to necessarily occurring.

nihilism. From the Latin, *nihilo* (nothing); a philosophical worldview denying the existence of an after-life and/or any ultimate accountability such as God.

out-of-body experience. The feeling of being outside your body, usually accompanied by the sense that you can see your body from an external perspective.

psychosomatic. Bodily condition(s) caused by the mind, such as worrying yourself sick.

Rituale Romanum. Roman Catholic liturgical book, first published in 1614. The services were significantly altered following the Second Vatican Council (1962–65).

spiritist. One who regularly seeks to contact the dead or claims to communicate with spirits.

stigmata. An event whereby a person receives a copy or duplication of the five wounds of Christ upon his or her own body.

stigmatic. One who has claimed to have received the five wounds of the stigmata.

supernaturalism. A philosophical worldview asserting that there is existence "above" nature such as spiritual or divine beings.